Four Letter Words:

A Collection of Poems by G.T. Hoffman

Table of Contents

When is Enough, Enough?

Captain

Betrayed

Freak

Dream Realities

By Death (Do We Part)

Masking Misery

Drunk

Demented

Do You Know?

Words Fail Me

Mentor

Little Things

Paradise

The Birth of A World

Winter's Rose

For My Sister

Raindrops

War Cry

And Now

Between

Broken

Empty

Beneath the Green

10,000 Steps

When is Enough, Enough?

I ponder as I sit, I sit as I ponder

How did life come to this? Silently, I wonder.

I stand as I think, I think as I stand

Why did I drift so far? I had a good plan.

I break as I heal, I heal as I break

How could they know? There's no sound I make.

I cry as they label, they label as I cry

Why can't they understand? Not one dries my eye.

I am flawed to perfection, but perfection is flawed

How can we be unified? Love is outlawed.

I strive as I fail, I fail as I strive

Why is this the only meaning? What it means to be alive.

I wait as time passes, time passes as I wait

How have we still not changed? It will soon be too late.

I crumble as they point, they point as I crumble

Why don't they help? They only turn from the rubble.

I hate what I love, I love what I hate

How could I change? It is my fate.

I am tough to be careful, I am careful to be tough

Why will no one else say it? Enough is enough.

Captain

   Eyes, deeper than the calm seas, have
a gravity pull stronger than the
Moon's on the tides. Tell me, how do I
keep myself from drowning?
   Sworn to never let anchor fall— too afraid
to rest within these waves' turmoil.
   Tossed between shaky dreams and shifting
realities; Eros, have mercy on me.
   Tormented with swells of desire— praying
for this voyage to expire. Tempting
the stars and my luck; navigating these wild
waves while uninspired and stuck.
   Destination is lost within a fog of emotion.
   Judgement hazes further with
each day upon this angry ocean— turning
back has never been an option.
   Poseidon preserve my Captain until love has
proven to be stronger than the fearful
pull of my raging seas. My shore abides with
him forevermore.

Betrayed

Betrayed by the fragility of my own heart, and

       wounds that are

Racked by aftershocks of the bitterly applied salt-

       the skies grew

Ominous as my soul helplessly watched the Fall. My tongue,

       bitten red, and

Kept silent by the mere might of my mind; overwhelmed

       by waves, and

Endless plagues- released mantras of why? My

       anchor has failed;

Neptune had no mercy to be felt, and I'm left to drift

       Love's unforgiving swells.

Freak

Fierce like lightning in a blizzard.

White hot rods pierce

Through a frozen atmosphere.

Nothing is clear for comprehension.

A calm will come again.

My anger no longer makes sense.

Snow disappears. Spring reappears.

With it comes a great flood

That will cover all the forgotten years.

It's just a freak happening

It'll never happen again.

Or so they thought, and so did I.

Dream Realities

Have you ever suffered a dream that so
mimicked reality, that you need to be
reminded it was not a memory, but a
wonderful wish indeed?

Yet, I wish not for this one to repeat.
It brought pain and caused my heart to
bleed. By night he came, full of a luminous love
like a furious flame, and the danger I dared not heed.

His eyes shone bright and proved to be
deep—deeper than every sea. I swooned in
his arms, as they first made me weak— then strong,
and provided my every want— then need.

I awoke with a start, but he
had already played his part and planted
the poisonous seed. I stood by helpless
as he stole my heart with a sickening speed.

I was oblivious to his plan, until he
had already completed his deed. Is it not
enough that he haunts my dreams when
I sleep? Must he also torture me when I am awake?

The greatest horror— I have come to
believe— is when we can find no escape
through sleep from our lightless realities,
nor our darkened dreams.

By Death (Do We Part)

One frosted window up on a faraway hill;

Too far to see within, but light shines through still.

My love, my life, resides there; however,

My body, my soul, must lie here forever.

To be separated by time, by water, and air;

A pain that is nearly too much to bare.

My broken body shall never heal,

So I stare at the hope beyond that window sill.

The lake between is cursed with winter's chill;

Its brackish depths are undisturbed, until

Spring's sweet spirit returns to the air,

And warm sunlight falls upon my Love's hair.

A broken bench, and a rotting chair

Separates the two hearts living here, living there.

One's in the frosted window up on the faraway hill;

However, mine must lie here; forever silent and still.

Masking Misery

I shake yes, but say no.
I say no
with a voice, in that place
where only I can go.
        They see a smile, hear a
        laugh— to them, this means that
        The Storm has passed.
"She'll be fine, now. It's over, at last."
They nod.
They nod with assurance— blind to
the shadows still being cast.
        My heart weighs too much
        to care, and my mind is worn
        more than a favorite chair.
My soul betrays me. It
is weak.
It is weak for food that doesn't
fulfill my real need.
        I hide this from their eyes, but
        they are already fooled by my
        disguise, of total bliss.

Drunk

Your smile remains present—
Perhaps even more so than before
but your eyes are now empty,
because you have left my world.
You were so strong. Your love
was pure. The lone light of my
life— I was sure. Now you have
fallen, and our love is forgotten.
Your words are sluggish—
Loving promises made into complete
rubbish. My eyes are wrung dry. There is
no peace for my tired soul to hope to find.
With unsteady steps you
cross over the boundaries— unspoken,
but understandably there. Each footfall
is taken without heed or care.
I'll walk away broken, yet with my pride
intact. You won't be able to say
the same— tomorrow perhaps— when
you have to look back.

Demented

Tricky
how you always say almost.
Stubborn.
My heart refuses to run.
Quiet,
because you never want to boast.
Demented.
I think your games are fun.

Lonely
you never say the right words.
Angry.
I'm not good enough for you.
Caged,
we're stuck like flightless birds.
Demented.
I believe every word you *do say* is true.

Fleeting
our time together is never enough.
Faking.
I pretend it doesn't hurt.
Scarred,
from conversations a little too tough.
Demented.
I still wear your baseball shirt.

Blindly
I handed you a whole heart.
Unaware.
I stood faithful as you tore it apart.
Smug,
you seem to feel so smart.
Demented.
I am still willing to restart.

Do You Know?

Like an engine my heart beats faster

every single time I hear

your uniquely beautiful laughter.

Do you know that I love you? Like a pup following her master

and always lending an ear—

eager to do what is asked of her.

Do you know that I miss you?

Like a storm beginning to gather, and bringing dark shadows of

fear—

your warm smile makes them scatter.

Do you know that l need you? Like a novel without ending

chapters—

incomplete if you're not here; only your smile truly matters.

Do you believe in my love for you?

Words Fail Me

Words fail me,

as reminiscent thoughts overwhelm me

with waves of wishful thoughts

and tides of "what ifs" that constantly ail me.

Was I wrong to say goodbye? If the power

to turn back time was mine

Could I? Would I?

Explain my reasons, and therefore think back to

Sweeter seasons than these?

Take me back to those too few

days of innocent bliss.

But love has ran its course—

the destruction path is more than enough

to endorse the theology of a broken heart.

Regretfully I admit to my

unknowingly evil part.

My ugly deeds cling to me, like grabbling weeds—

they hang off my face

for the world to see. Oh, how can I explain!

When words fail me?

Mentor

Mirror mirror in the hall
To you alone, my mentor, does all beauty belong.
The image you show me
Is not my own. Still similarities remain.

You'll show me my future.
Steer me away from your past.
In beauty and grace you teach me
How to make life work for us instead.

You're haunted by memories
Unknown and unseen by these eyes.
Do you truly believe that you can change what
You see when you look at me?

I want to be everything that you have
So graciously unveiled before me.
The mirror I found in the hall
That owns all the beauty of this century.

Paradise

Perfect waves, crimson-tipped, the sunset simmering.
Where cooling sand caresses toes, and time
stands still. A breeze that kisses faces,
and a bird song most beautiful
of all the ages. This is it.
Or might it be:
A long walk with a
lover, kissing slightly before
leaving home for work, holding one
another so tightly that we lose all notions of
being two bodies instead one. Knowing the difference in
breathing that means awake, asleep, dreaming; hearing music in
a heartbeat that lullabies can only
 keep mimicking. Isn't this it?

The Birth of a World

"I'm coming,"

the world whispered from its womb.

"Prepare my chariot— I'll be there soon!"

Golden rays of the Sun, mixed with the breath of the Moon,

created a royal carpet vibrating with a joyous tune.

It was all this, and more, that she heard as she sat,

beneath the pear tree; youth still in her lap.

"The world is coming," the bees seemed to say.

"Are you ready to see it today?"

Winter's Rose

Her beauty was unparalleled— causing his heart to fail.

She once had seen a majestic king, now suddenly, she

knew his every twisted dream, hidden weakness, and

dwarfed reality. Her knowledge grew— love left

her heart's room, and a rigid fragile rose was

all that could ever bloom in the

shadows of her soul.

For My Sister

Do you remember when we
played pretend in the yard
way back then?

We were brave explorers, even
eagles couldn't have out-soared
us. Climbing the highest mountains,
swimming the deepest seas;
we were the best chefs in our
own mud-pie bakery.

I think of our days in the sun, when
all we knew was mischief and fun. If
my days are low, my mind will always
go to you.

When we planned our futures so grand,
filled with Prince Charmings, matching
castles, always side by side.

Now we walk similarly different
paths, time's wrath trying our bonds,
stealing our wands, but we will
still go on.

For what the world cannot see, and
perhaps cannot understand, is the enormity
of a sister's love.

It is grand enough to stretch across oceans,
time, and mountain tops. A sister's love
never stops.

My greatest wish, in my heart and soul,
is that you find happiness, no matter
where you go.

Love,
Your Sister

Raindrops

Floating spheres of life,
        Revolving endless, in and of yourselves
Glistening sparks inside darkness;
        An awaiting salvation on our behalf.

Do we notice?
Do we appreciate?

We run as if with fright-
        Speak with hate: 'go away!'
Missing what cannot be seen
        We ignore life's necessity.

War Cry

Jolted awake by the strobes
and the screams
as she thrusted her way
through the small bedroom window.
Nerves were on end, hands
sticky with sweat, and heart rates
 out the roof, as we tried
to use muggled minds to make sense
of the scene. "It's just a little thunder,"
was said in attempt to ease,
but this was nothing like the normal
banging of Heaven's floors. These
were sounds of anger, of warning,
or even threat of something
much worse to come if not heeded
 and understood. Thoughts swelled
through our minds in fear of
the night terrors:
we've been bombed...

No it's only thunder,

but not like any kind before,

almost like Mother Nature is furious.

Little Things

It's these, that reminds us of the whole picture:

The direction each hair
 is combed down,
The unchecked, high flying,
laugh that shakes the entirety of you,
The inability to entertain
the slightest possibility of failure,
The unending faith in me, even
when I have none,
The innocence of your smile
 when I kiss your dreams,
Waking to find you holding me,
The wrinkles on your nose
when you giggle,
You're the sum of so much more:
The feeling of your hand in mine,
Hearing your voice
pulling me from nightmares,
Your simple joy of the little things,
A smile meant
To say what words cannot touch,
Knowing you are mine.
This image of you seems bare
 when compared to life;
 however, it is the polaroid stamped
  onto my soul and mind.

And Now

Once I knew you, I couldn't forget. The flutters
 made you much more real,
then the photographs on the screen.
My heart and mind melted a little
more in sync with the
whoosh whoosh whoosh whoosh lullaby.
That sound that I lived for and would've died by. Within you,
I found a tiny piece of me. So many worries, plans,
and thoughts swirled before you were
brought into this world. They all left
the moment I saw your tiny and swollen face. Your true face
was the most beautiful I'd ever seen. I knew then,
and now more so that you will tell me
just who you were born to be.
Only I must wait
patiently.

Between

Not one, or two, maybe three or
four – it could be even more. Of course,
it never mattered to me before, until someone
said it should. Like, why do I sound
southern, but look hood? I like fried chicken,
but not if I have to take it off the bone.
I'm tall, but I can't really play
any type of ball – singing is my true passion. I
have really terrible fashion. What happens
when someone cute walks by; does it have to matter
the color of their skin, hair and eyes?

Sick of hearing, "you're beautiful the
way you are" when yesterday I was told
my hair was sticking out too far. The glances
are not comfortable, and I wish to be small,
but that was not the cards given, nope –
not at all. Too fair to fit with this crowd, and too
dark to blend into the background. Where do I
go now? My kind doesn't have a name – only a title
and sometimes we also take the blame
for things out of our control. It wasn't us who
took the genetic dice for a roll.

So label me 'other,' if that's what is easier
for you to do. I'll find a name someday
and it won't come from you. For now, I will
answer to one thing, a name I choose, and I
will make a home here – between option
one and option two.

Broken

Beckon me closer with fierce ice that pierces
my soul when your eyes lock onto mine. Burn my body
with the heat from your own, and heal me with
nectar from your lips as they caress my name. Bury me
with the weight of your words – three words.
Burden my mind with unholy thoughts and memories of
those sleepless nights. Break me to pieces,
please, just one more time.

Empty
-containing nothing; not filled or occupied

Alone, it felt as though only God
would want to watch the unraveling
on the floor. Clenched
in a fist gone white
from the pressure, was an outfit – more of
a dream made material. Light as air;
yet soul crushing, heart crunching
when nothing was there
to fill it.

Somewhere deep a cry
began to rise up
and out, turning into a wail
and a sob. That tiny bundle of fabric
alone staunching the flow.
While kneeling, still clenching, a prayer
escaped cracked lips:
Let whoever fills this
know they are loved so deep
and immense; never leave them as
empty or void of bliss.

Beneath the Green

Dreaming isn't meant to be

done alone.

I've gotten lost many times

doing that,

searching all around me,

Still, why am I looking beneath the green?

Our masks are good, letting show only

what we deem should. Even the best are

fatally flawed, with cracks,

dents from victoriously vicious claws.

A deep darkness fights

for a way in between these,

a light from within

shines so that no one achieves

what lies hidden beneath the green.

10,000 Steps

Pink sneakers. Runners.

Statement-makers. Hers.

Her favorite pair of shoes, just
sitting alone by the door, wanting to be filled, used,
abused. The last pavement they hit was more than two
years ago. Still can't throw them out though. These
pink, slightly stained running shoes, that she used to walk
into the hospital for a routine scan that didn't go as planned.

Made in the USA
Middletown, DE
18 April 2023